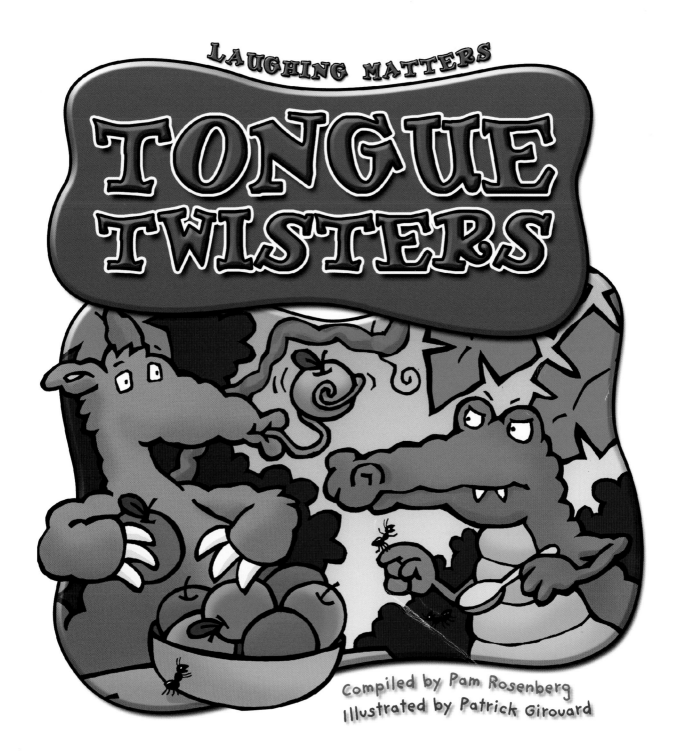

LAUGHING MATTERS

TONGUE TWISTERS

Compiled by Pam Rosenberg
Illustrated by Patrick Girouard

Special thanks to Katie Cottrell for her assistance in compiling source materials.

Published in the United States of America by The Child's World®
P.O. Box 326, Chanhassen, MN 55317-0326
800-599-READ
www.childsworld.com

Acknowledgments

The Child's World®: Mary Berendes, Publishing Director

Editorial Directions, Inc.: E. Russell Primm, Editorial Director and Line Editor; Katie Marsico, Assistant Editor; Matthew Messbarger, Editorial Assistant; Susan Hindman and Susan Ashley, Proofreaders

The Design Lab: Kathleen Petelinsek, Designer and Page Production

Library of Congress Cataloging-in-Publication Data

Rosenberg, Pam.
  Tongue twisters / compiled by Pam Rosenberg ; illustrated by Patrick Girouard.
      p. cm. — (Laughing matters)
Summary: Simple tongue twisters grouped by subjects such as places, travel, kids, and school.
  ISBN 1-59296-078-2 (alk. paper)
  1. Tongue twisters. [1. Tongue twisters.] I. Girouard, Patrick, ill. II. Title. III. Series.
  PN6371.5.R59 2004
  818'.602—dc22   2003018091

ANIMALS

Ten tiny turtles sitting on a tiny tin tub turned tan.

Ann Anteater ate Andy Alligator's apples, so angry Andy Alligator ate Ann Anteater's ants.

Ape cakes, grape cakes.

Three blind mice blew bugles.

How much wood would a woodchuck chuck if a woodchuck could chuck wood?

The sixth sheik's sixth sheep's sick.

As the roaring rocket rose, the restless roosters rollicked.

A fly and a flea in a flue were imprisoned, so what could they do? Said the fly, "Let us flee!" "Let us fly!" said the flea. And they flew through the flaw in the flue. Said the flea to the fly as he flew through the flue, "There's a flaw in the floor of the flue." Said the fly to the flea as he flew through the flue, "A flaw in the floor of the flue doesn't bother me. Does it bother you?"

A big black bug bit a big black bear, made the big black bear bleed blood.

How high would a horsefly fly if a horsefly would fly high?

Big black bugs bleed blue black blood but baby black bugs bleed blue blood.

The blue bluebird blinks.

Mares eat oats and does eat oats but little lambs eat ivy, a kid will eat ivy too, wouldn't you?

The cat catchers can't catch caught cats.

Cows graze in droves on grass that grows on grooves in groves.

5

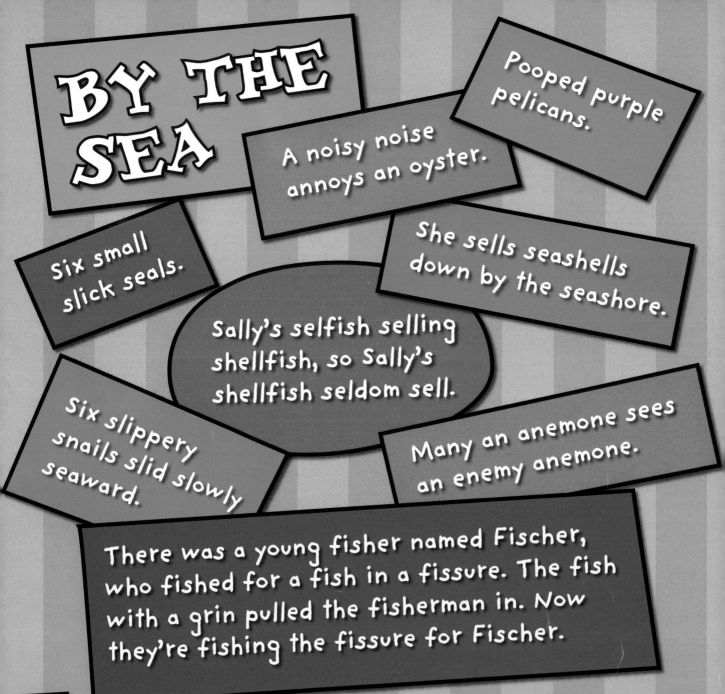

BY THE SEA

Pooped purple pelicans.

A noisy noise annoys an oyster.

Six small slick seals.

She sells seashells down by the seashore.

Sally's selfish selling shellfish, so Sally's shellfish seldom sell.

Six slippery snails slid slowly seaward.

Many an anemone sees an enemy anemone.

There was a young fisher named Fischer, who fished for a fish in a fissure. The fish with a grin pulled the fisherman in. Now they're fishing the fissure for Fischer.

Five fat frogs fled from fifty fierce fish.

Six smart sharp sharks.

Which is the witch that wished the wicked wish?

A ghost's sheets would soon shrink in such suds.

Amidst the mists and coldest frosts, with stoutest wrists and loudest boasts, he thrusts his fist against the posts and still insists he sees the ghosts.

I wish to wish the wish you wish to wish, but if you wish the wish the witch wishes, I won't wish the wish you wish to wish.

If two witches would watch two watches, which witch would watch which watch?

Each Easter Eddie eats eighty Easter eggs.

Shy Sheila shakes soft shimmering silks.

Peggy Babcock.

Old oily Ollie oils old oily autos.

Elmer Arnold.

Roy Wayne.

Gertie's great-grandma grew aghast at Gertie's grammar.

Will you, William?

Raise Ruth's red roof.

Friendly Frank flips fine flapjacks.

Sly Sam slurps Sally's soup.

Literally literary literature.

I can't stand when it's written rotten.

A tutor who tooted a flute died to tutor two tooters to toot. Said the two to the tutor, "Is it harder to toot, or to tutor two tooters to toot?"

He threw three free throws.

White eraser? Right away, sir!

Pick a partner and practice passing, for if you pass proficiently, perhaps you'll play professionally.

Purple paper people.

The boy blinked at the blank bank blackboard.

Rolling red wagons.

A knapsack strap.

Pug puppy.

Mommy made me mash my M&Ms.

Kinky kite kits.

Penny's pretty pink piggy bank.

There's no need to light a night-light on a light night like tonight. For a night-light's just a slight light on a light night like tonight.

Yanking yellow yo-yos.

15

FOOD AND COOKING

Blake the baker bakes black bread.

Betty Botter bought a bit of butter. "But," said she, "this butter's bitter. If I put it in my batter, it will make my batter bitter. But a bit of better butter that would make my batter better." So Betty Botter bought a bit of better butter and she put it in her bitter batter and made her bitter batter a bit better.

The cute cookie cutters cut cute cookies. Did the cute cookie cutters cut cute cookies? If the cute cookie cutters cut cute cookies, where are the cute cookies the cute cookie cutters cut?

Peter Piper picked a peck of pickled peppers.
A peck of pickled peppers Peter Piper picked.
If Peter Piper picked a peck of pickled peppers,
how many pickled peppers did Peter Piper pick?

An oyster met an oyster, and they were oysters two. Two oysters met two oysters, and they were oysters too. Four oysters met a pint of milk and they were oyster stew.

A canner exceedingly canny, one morning remarked to his granny, "A canner can anything that he can, but a canner can't can a can, can he?"

17

Tuesday is stew day. Stew day is Tuesday.

Does double bubble gum double bubble?

For fine fresh fish, phone Phil.

Lotty licks lollies lolling in the lobby.

Six sticky sucker sticks.

Crisp crusts crackle crunchily.

Chop shops stock chops.

Lily ladles little Letty's lentil soup.

Shredded Swiss cheese.

She brews a proper cup of coffee in a copper coffee-pot.

Greek grapes.

PLACES/ TRAVEL

Beautiful babbling brooks bubble between blossoming banks.

Cheap ship trip.

We surely shall see the sun shine soon.

Betty and Bob brought back blue balloons from the big bazaar.

Thieves seize skis.

Sure, the ship's shipshape, sir.

A pleasant place to place a plaice is a place where a plaice is pleased to be placed.

A bloke's back bike brake block broke.

Mrs. Smith's fish sauce shop.

20

The sawingest saw I ever saw saw was the saw I saw saw in Arkansas.

Shelter for six sick scenic sightseers.

The two-twenty-two train tore through the tunnel.

Andy ran from the Andes to the Indies in his undies.

The sinking steamer sank.

Stagecoach stops.

Are our oars okay?

Unique New York.

Truly rural.

MISCELLANEOUS THINGS

Yellow leather, yellow feather.

Flash message.

Switch watch, wrist-watch.

The sun shines on shop signs.

Please pay promptly.

Preshrunk silk shirts.

Sam's shop stocks short, spotted socks.

22

About Patrick Girouard:

Patrick Girouard has been illustrating books for almost 15 years but still looks remarkably lifelike. He loves reading, movies, coffee, robots, a beautiful red-haired lady named Rita, and especially his sons, Marc and Max. Here's an interesting fact: A dog named Sam lives under his drawing board. You can visit him (Patrick, not Sam) at www.pgirouard.com.

About Pam Rosenberg:

Pam Rosenberg is a former junior high school teacher and corporate trainer. She currently works as an author, editor, and the mother of Sarah and Jake. She took on this project as a service to all her fellow parents of young children. At least now their kids will have lots of jokes to choose from when looking for the one they will tell their parents over and over and over again!